THE POEMS OF SULPICIA

The Poems of Sulpicia

TRANSLATED BY

JOHN HEATH-STUBBS

LONDON: HEARING EYE

First published in this edition 2000
by Hearing Eye, 99 Torriano Avenue,
London NW5 2RX
Printed in Great Britain by Peter Lloyd
at The Holbeche Press, Rugby
Translation © John Heath-Stubbs, 2000
Illustration © Emily Johns, 2000
ISBN 1 870841 66 2

INTRODUCTION

Classical Greece had several notable women poets—Sappho above all, but also Corinna, Erinna and Anyte. Sadly, their work has only come down to us in fragments. We have perhaps only one complete poem of Sappho and a number of quotations by grammarians or literary critics. In the last hundred years or so, further scraps have turned up in the sands of Egypt—poems from books which must have been consigned to the rubbish tip. There is some evidence indeed that Sappho's poems were deliberately suppressed by Christian authorities, because of the frankness of their eroticism. Corinna and Erinna survive only in fragments of a similar provenance. Anyte has a handful of short poems included in the Greek Anthology (see: *The Poems of Anyte*, translated by John Heath-Stubbs and Carol Whiteside—Greville Press, 1976) but we know that she also wrote some narrative poems of considerable length. When it comes to the Latin literature of Rome there is only one woman poet's name recorded and that is Sulpicia. The eight poems here translated are included in book four of the works of the poet Tibullus (60–19 BC) along with some others attributed to members of Tibullus's circle, including Sulpicia's lover Cerinthus. In addition to these there is a group of poems known as "the garland of Sulpicia". These may well have been written by Tibullus or possibly Ovid. I have translated two of them—one on Cerinthus's pig-sticking and one in which Sulpicia gives thanks for his birthday. This is for their intrinsic interest, and also because we do seem to hear in them an echo of Sulpicia's authentic voice, if only at one remove.

Martial (circa 43–104 AD), more than a century later, says that chaste virgins and virtuous matrons read the poems of Sulpicia. He is apparently not being sarcastic at this point, but the description hardly fits the poems of Sulpicia that we have. There may therefore have been two Sulpicias, or—a rather depressing thought—Tibullus's friend may have dwindled into respectability in her later years.

Nineteenth-century Latin scholars, for the most part refused to believe that Sulpicia was the author of the poems attributed to her and thought that Tibullus wrote them for her. Oxford and Cambridge dons, or German professors, they knew little, one feels, about women and were reluctant to believe that any woman could or should write poems so passionately outspoken as these are. This was the age when the great German scholar, Wilamowitz, sought to persuade the world that Sappho was simply the headmistress of a select finishing school for well-connected young ladies of the Lesbian isle. If, as these older scholars said, the style of the poems closely resembles that of Tibullus, this is no argument against Sulpicia's authorship. It seems to be the case that she was a member of Tibullus's circle and she would naturally pick up his style. But these poems seem to me—and I have of course no pretension to scholarship whatsoever—to show an idiosyncratic tendency to turn back on themselves in an interesting and complex way which is hardly that of Tibullus.

All that we know about Sulpicia can be deduced from the poems. She was a member of the aristocratic Sulpician clan and enjoyed considerable sexual freedom, although under the tutelage of her guardian, Messala. One must remember that Roman women were always under such tutelage—either that of their fathers, their elder brothers, their sons or their husbands or some other guardian. In translating her I have tried to make her speak to our own time, though attempting to render the Latin as accurately as possible. I have not imitated the original elegiac metre or used any conventional English metre. But I have availed myself of the metrical freedom open to English poets since the days of Ezra Pound and T. S. Eliot. I have naturally had Ezra Pound in mind, notably his *Homage to Sextus Propertius*, but I hope I have not followed his example in perpetuating mistranslations—due either to carelessness or sometimes to a desire to play a joke on his readers. The Latin text I have used is that of Postgate in the Loeb Classical Library (1913). I have also used his accompanying prose translations and have consulted some others including the old Bohn Library, and the Penguin edition edited by Philip Dunlop.

JOHN HEATH-STUBBS

CERINTHUS GOES PIG-STICKING

Leave the boy alone, wild boar
Whether you haunt the lush pasture lands
Or the intricate corners of hanging woods on the hills
Don't whet your tusks for the fight
But send him back safe to me. Let not Diana
Lead him astray through his love of hunting.
Let forests wither quite and dogs become extinct!
Are you out of your mind to injure your soft hands
Weaving a toil in thorny places round the quarry?
What's the point of sneaking into wild beasts' dens
And scratching your white legs with bramble prickles?
But if I could come with you, Cerinthus, I'd carry the nets
Over the mountains and track the prints of the deer,
And let loose the hounds undoing their iron collars.
I'd get to like the forest if I remembered
I'd lain in your arms beside the tackle.
Then let the boar come up to the nets indeed—
He can go scot free if he doesn't disturb our lovemaking.
But without me, forget about sex—obey Diana
And spread the nets, chaste youth with chaste hands.
And any girl who might happen to intrude on our love nook
May she meet up with wild beasts herself and be torn to bits.
You can leave all this hunting to your father,
Come back as quick as you like into my arms.

CERINTHUS' BIRTHDAY

This day which granted life to you for my sake
Let it always be for me a festal day.
This day the Fates decreed new slavery for women
Bestowing on you sovereignty of their hearts.
I burn more fiercely than the rest, but gladly
If you too burn for me with an equal flame.
May passion like mine be yours too
From our secret joys, from our eyes, from your guardian spirit.
Good guardian spirit, gather up this pinch of incense
Look favourably upon my prayers, but only if
His pulse beats quicker when he thinks of me.
But if even now he is thinking of someone else,
Spirit, I pray you, quit his faithless hearth.
Venus, play fair, let each of us
Be equally enslaved or else
Strike off these shackles from me. Rather
Let each of us be bound with a tight bond
No future day shall break. The young man wishes
The same things I do, but doesn't want to
Blurt it out too openly. Presiding spirit,
Then, grant this prayer—what does it matter
If he speaks it out or not?

IT'S OUT AT LAST

Love has come at last. The very idea
That I'd hide it makes me more ashamed
Than openly confessing. Won over
By my Muse's supplication, Cythera's Goddess
Has brought him to me, placed him in my arms.
What Venus promised, she has fulfilled.
Let them tattle who have missed their chance.
I'll not entrust the news to a sealed letter
That none may read of it before my lover does.
I loathe to wear a mask in deference
To what the world may say. Let everyone hear
That we have come together—each of us
Deserving the other.

SULPICIA'S BIRTHDAY

My dreaded birthday is looming, and I've got to spend it
There in the odious country without Cerinthus.
What is more agreeable than the city? Is a country estate
A fit place for a girl or the fields
By the cold river Arno? Stop fussing about me
Messala, my kinsman, you're much too ready
To take me on an unnecessary journey.
Carried hence—I leave my soul and my senses behind
As I cannot exercise my own free will.

SHE CAN BE AT ROME, AFTER ALL

Don't you know that the burden of an unnecessary journey
Is lifted from your poor girl's heart?
I can be at Rome, it now seems, for my birthday—
This comes to you by an unexpected stroke of luck.

CERINTHUS IS UNFAITHFUL

I am glad you think you can get away with this
Allowing yourself a liberty at my expense—
That a togged-up tart with a wool basket
Is worthier of your attentions than Sulpicia
Daughter of Servius though she be.
Others care about me and are indignant
On my behalf that I must give place
To a low-born bit of stuff such as she is.

SULPICIA IS ILL

Cerinthus, have you any feelings now
For your poor girl while a fever
Racks her and torments her weakened body?
I should not want to overcome this illness
Unless I thought you would wish it too.
What would be the good of my recovering
If you could put up with my sufferings easily?

SULPICIA REGRETS

Light of my being, let me not be so passionately
Desired by you as I guess I was some days since
If in the whole of my young years
I ever did anything quite so silly,
As I think it was
When I left you on your own the other night,
Hoping to hide the fierceness of the passion
That all the time was burning within me.